MODERN WARFARE

Sea Warfare

By Martin J. Dougherty

Please visit our Web site www.garethstevens.com. For a free color catalog of all our high-quality books, call toll free 1-800-542-2595 or fax 1-877-542-2596.

Library of Congress Cataloging-in-Publication Data

Dougherty, Martin J.
    Sea warfare / by Martin J. Dougherty.
        p. cm. _ (Modern warfare)
    Includes bibliographical references and index.
    ISBN-10: 1-4339-2734-9   ISBN-13: 978-1-4339-2734-8 (lib. bdg.)
    1. Naval art and science_Juvenile literature. 2. Warships_Juvenile literature. 3. Sea-power_
Juvenile literature. I. Title.
V109.D68   2010
359_dc22   2009019091

This North American edition first published in 2010 by
Gareth Stevens Publishing
111 East 14th Street, Suite 349
New York, NY 10003

Copyright © 2010 by Amber Books, Ltd.
Produced by Amber Books Ltd., Bradley's Close
74–77 White Lion Street
London N1 9PF, U.K.

Amber Project Editor: James Bennett
Amber Copy Editors: Melanie Gray, Jim Mezzanotte
Amber Designer: Andrew Easton
Amber Picture Research: Terry Forshaw, Natascha Spargo

Gareth Stevens Executive Managing Editor: Lisa M. Herrington
Gareth Stevens Editor: Joann Jovinelly
Gareth Stevens Senior Designer: Keith Plechaty

Interior Images
BAE Systems: 18
Military Visualizations, Inc.: 1, 19
U.S. Coast Guard: 26, 27, 28, 29
U.S. Department of Defense: 3, 4 (U.S. Navy), 5 (U.S. Navy), 6 (U.S. Navy), 7 (both U.S. Navy), 8 (U.S. Navy), 9, 10 (U.S. Navy), 11 (U.S. Navy), 12 (U.S. Navy), 13 (U.S. Navy), 14 (all U.S. Navy), 15 (U.S. Navy), 16 (U.S. Navy), 17, 20 (U.S. Navy), 21, 22, 23 (U.S. Navy), 24, 25

Cover Images
Front cover: U.S. Department of Defense

Printed in the United States of America

CPSIA Compliance Information: Batch #CR011090GS: For further information contact Gareth Stevens, New York, New York at 1-800-542-2595

▶ MISSILE LAUNCH
A Trident ballistic missile is launched from the nuclear-powered submarine USS *Ohio*.

CONTENTS

CHAPTER 1

FORCES AT SEA

Navies do many important jobs. They fight sea battles, but they also help fight battles on land and in the air. Their ships travel across oceans. They move people and weapons around the globe.

A navy usually has fast, powerful warships. It often has other ships, too. Navies may have submarines. Some have **aircraft carriers**. Navies also carry supplies or patrol along coasts.

A Group Effort

Most navy ships work together as a group. Each ship has a job it does best. A large group of ships is called a **fleet**. In the U.S. Navy, each fleet works together in a certain part of the world.

Part of a navy is on land. That part keeps track of all ships, people, and supplies. It trains the sailors who work on the ships. It also repairs ships so they work well.

▼ CARRIER STRIKE GROUP
The USS *Enterprise* (*front, center*) is a U.S. aircraft carrier. Some of the ships around it are armed with missiles. They will protect the carrier if an enemy attacks.

Vital Support

Some navy ships do not fight. Instead, they help other ships that do the fighting. They bring supplies to warships. Without those supplies, the warships would have to return to land. Navy ships supply troops in different parts of the world.

Navies have medical ships. Those ships are like hospitals. During land battles, helicopters bring injured soldiers to the hospital ships. Hospital ships also offer help after disasters, such as storms or earthquakes.

In the Navy

Before taking part in missions, new sailors go through tough training. After that training, they learn a particular job. They might

▲ FULLY LOADED
Warships need supplies of ammunition and food for the crew. Those items must be loaded before the ship can set sail.

DID YOU KNOW?
A navy ship often has letters in front of its name. U.S. ships have the letters "USS." They stand for "United States Ship."

operate weapons, or they might help guide a ship.

Navy officers go to a special college. Then they become leaders. On a ship, the captain is the officer in charge. All sailors follow the captain's orders. The captain follows orders from another officer who is in charge of many ships.

Sailor Life

Sailors may not see land for months. They often work long hours aboard the ship. When the ship returns to land, they get time

▼ TAKE COMFORT
The USS *Comfort* is a hospital ship that can go anywhere in the world. Hospital ships often help people when there is a disaster.

The USS *Comfort* has a big red cross on it so that it does not get attacked. International laws protect hospital ships, even during war.

▶ TRAINING SHIP

The USS *Trayer* is a training ship that is inside a large building. When the ship is "attacked," the floors tilt and there is fake smoke. Recruits have to stay up all night putting out "fires," moving ammunition to safety, and rescuing other sailors. Training is exhausting. After training, the sailors are ready for real emergencies.

▼ SAILORS ON PARADE

Sailors are on parade aboard the USS *Boxer*. They stand at attention ready to be inspected. A high-ranking officer is going to check that they are properly dressed and ready to do their jobs. He will also check that the ship is in good condition.

off, which is called "leave." Then they must go back to the ship.

Like soldiers and marines, sailors wear uniforms. They have plain uniforms for work. They also have fancy dress uniforms for special events. Sailors wear **insignia**, too. Those badges show what **rank** they hold and what job they do.

SEALS

A few U.S. sailors become Navy SEALs. "SEAL" is short for sea, air, land. Those sailors go wherever they are needed. They do the most dangerous jobs.

To become Navy SEALs, sailors go through difficult training. That training lasts more than two years. SEALs must be able to

▲ FLOATING SUPPLY TRUCK
This cargo ship carries ammunition and other supplies for the fighting ships. It sends them whatever they need using helicopters before going back to port to get more supplies.

IN THEIR OWN WORDS

"By the end of their time here, the [SEAL] students know that they can be wet and cold and sandy and still do what it is they need to do. Uncomfortable does not mean stop. It means you are uncomfortable but still doing your job."

U.S. Navy Lt. Frederick Martin with the Naval Special Warfare Center, Coronado, CA

swim 50 meters (164 feet) underwater without taking a breath. Many sailors do not pass that test.

SEALs learn how to fight on land and in water. They also learn underwater **demolition**. Navy SEALs sneak into enemy territory. They may come in by parachute, or they may swim underwater to shore. Once on land, they do their jobs. Then they get out fast!

Camouflaged hats such as these help SEALs sneak up on the enemy without being spotted. In a jungle stream, the colors on the hat blend in with leaves and mud.

DID YOU KNOW?

There are only a few thousand Navy SEALs. For them, teamwork is very important. A Navy SEAL has never been left behind or taken prisoner.

▼ UNDERWATER WARRIORS

These U.S. Navy SEALs are training to attack an enemy by swimming underwater. The soldier in front has a grenade launcher underneath his M16 rifle.

CHAPTER 2

AIRCRAFT CARRIERS

Fighter planes need runways for taking off and landing. But if the target is too far from the runway, the planes will run out of fuel before getting back.

Aircraft carriers are like floating runways. Those ships have long, flat tops, where planes take off and land. The ships go anywhere in the world, so the planes never run out of fuel. They can reach their targets more easily.

How They Work

An aircraft carrier has a **hull**, as all ships do. The hull is made of thick steel.

▼ SUPERCARRIER

A large aircraft carrier is called a **supercarrier**. The supercarriers of the U.S. Navy can take their airplanes anywhere they are needed. After a mission, the airplanes return to the carrier to await further instructions.

The carrier has powerful **radar**. The radar can spot enemies and control the airplanes. These masts are tall so that the radar can work over a long distance.

There is not much space on an aircraft carrier. Some airplanes have wings that fold up to take up less space on deck.

An aircraft carrier has many levels, or decks. One deck holds the engines. Another deck has living spaces for the crew. Planes are stored in the hangar deck.

The top level of an aircraft carrier is called the flight deck. Elevators take planes to it from the hangar deck. The flight deck also has a tall tower called an island. From here, officers can control the ship.

Cities at Sea

Aircraft carriers are huge. The U.S. Navy has the largest ones. Those ships are called supercarriers. They carry almost 100 aircraft. The ships rise 20 stories above the

▲ **READY TO FLY**
Airplanes are launched off the front of the carrier using powerful **catapults**. It takes about four seconds for an airplane to get airborne.

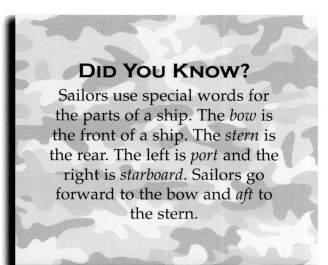

DID YOU KNOW?
Sailors use special words for the parts of a ship. The *bow* is the front of a ship. The *stern* is the rear. The left is *port* and the right is *starboard*. Sailors go forward to the bow and *aft* to the stern.

water. Supercarriers are longer than three football fields.

A supercarrier is sometimes called a city at sea. It can hold more than 5,000 sailors! A supercarrier runs on **nuclear power**. It can travel for several years without refueling.

Catapults and Hooks

Planes need long runways for taking off and landing. Even big aircraft carriers have runways that are too short, so the planes need help stopping. They use catapults and hooks.

The catapult works like a slingshot. It gets attached to the plane. Then, it flings the plane down the runway. Strong cables stretch across the flight deck. When the plane lands, a hook on its tail catches a cable.

▶ IN THE HANGAR
Sailors practice climbing up and down ropes inside the hangar of the USS *John C. Stennis*. They are surrounded by the carrier's aircraft. A supercarrier can carry up to 90 aircraft.

DID YOU KNOW?
The USS *Nimitz* is a supercarrier. On this ship, cooks serve 20,000 meals a day. Each week, the barbershop gives 1,500 haircuts. Each year, the post office handles one million pounds (453 tonnes) of mail.

On the Flight Deck

A flight deck is a busy place. Planes take off and land every 25 seconds! Some crews get planes ready to fly. Other crews guide the planes that land. Up in the tower, officers keep track of planes and crew.

Crews must be ready for emergencies. A plane might not hook a wire. Then it could crash or fall into the sea. Aircraft carriers have safety nets below the deck. A plane's jet might blow a sailor over the side!

IN THEIR OWN WORDS

"The flight deck is a dangerous place. It isn't enough just to look out for yourself … each of us needs to look out for our fellow shipmates."

Aviation Ordnance Airman George Frede aboard the USS *John C. Stennis*

▼ BUSY DECK

The catapult has just launched a fighter jet. Crew members rush to get it ready for the next one to launch. It is important to get each airplane into the air quickly. The flight deck might be needed for another airplane to land.

The catapult is powered by high-pressure steam from the ship's engines.

Aircraft carrier deck crews wear ear protection because the noise of the airplanes' engines is so loud.

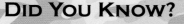

▲ TEAMWORK

Everyone works together to get the planes in the air. Some people pass messages. Some put missiles on planes. Others tell everyone when the planes are ready to launch. On U.S. aircraft carriers, crew members wear different colors depending on their jobs:

- Blue uniforms are worn by crew towing airplanes around the deck and operating the giant elevators, which bring airplanes up from the hangars.
- Red is worn by crew who handle weapons.
- Yellow is worn by officers in charge.
- Brown is worn by mechanics in charge of getting the airplanes ready to take off.
- Purple is worn by crew refueling the airplanes.
- Green uniforms are worn by many crew members, including catapult operators.
- White is worn by safety officers and medics.

DID YOU KNOW?

When a plane hits the flight deck, it is going fast. It is traveling 150 miles (241 kilometers) per hour. But when the hook catches, the plane stops in just two seconds!

Carriers in Action

Aircraft carriers mostly help with land battles. Planes take off from the ships and hit targets on land. The aircraft carriers can move around at sea, so they are harder to attack.

If the enemy does attack a carrier, it is ready. Carriers have big guns that fire very rapidly. They have missiles, too. Aircraft carriers put **decoys** in the water. If an enemy submarine fires a **torpedo**, it hits the decoy instead of the ship.

IN THEIR OWN WORDS

"Because landing on a carrier is more precise, Navy fliers smack the deck hard. If you try to flare your aircraft on the carrier [land softly], you either won't catch the trap wire, or you will catch it while you are still airborne ... [which is] very bad."

U.S. Navy Capt. Roger Pierce, EA-6B Prowler Pilot

▼ COMING IN TO LAND
This F/A-18 Hornet is about to land on an aircraft carrier. The hook hanging at the back is there to catch the wire stretched across the deck. That stops the plane in mere seconds.

CHAPTER 3

SUBMARINES

In most sea battles, the enemy can see a ship. But what if that ship is a **submarine**? Submarines mostly stay underwater. Subs dive deep beneath the surface. They stay hidden, traveling under the surface of the world's oceans. They hit targets at sea and on land.

IN THEIR OWN WORDS

"It felt like a training exercise until the first Tomahawk [cruise missile] was fired. The boat was moving vertically up and down. Everyone was looking around … it was one of the most exciting moments in our careers."

U.S. Navy Fire Controlman 2nd Class
(Submarine Service) Craig Lawrence
aboard the USS *Miami*

▼ ATTACK SUBMARINE
The USS *Louisville* is an attack submarine. It is shaped to slip quickly and quietly through the water. It can sneak up on enemies and take them by surprise.

This Trident missile has just been launched from the USS *Ohio*. This is a practice launch. Missiles such as this one can be launched from any ocean and can hit any target on land.

Best in Class

There are two kinds, or classes, of submarines. Attack submarines are built for sea battles. They fire torpedoes at ships and subs. Some also fire missiles at ships.

Missile subs hit targets on land. They carry nuclear missiles that fly long distances. Missile subs are larger than attack subs, but they are slower, too.

Submarines use **sonar** to find targets at sea. Sonar sends sound waves through water. Those sound waves hit enemy ships. Then, the sound waves bounce back to the sub. They let sailors know where enemies are hiding.

Up and Down

A submarine has **ballast tanks**. When those tanks are filled with air, the sub floats. When they fill with water, it dives. A sub carries extra air. When it needs to rise, air goes into the ballast tanks.

Hydroplanes stick out from the sub's sides. They are like small wings that tilt. They control how steeply a sub dives or rises. They also help the sub stay level.

Parts of a Sub

A small tower called a **sail** sticks up from the center of a sub. The sail holds the **periscope**. The periscope can stick up out of the water. It lets sailors see, but stay hidden. Today, some subs use cameras instead of periscopes.

▲ HIGH AND DRY
Engineers are getting this British Royal Navy submarine ready to launch. Its job is to hunt down enemy ships and submarines and sink them with torpedoes.

DID YOU KNOW?
A missile is a "smart" rocket. It can find targets on its own. A torpedo is similar to a missile. Instead of flying through the air, it travels through the water. Then it finds enemy ships or subs.

The sub's control room is located below the sail. In this area, sailors control the sub. The engine is usually in back. A sub has places for sailors to eat and sleep. It has air tanks so sailors can breathe. It also has equipment that turns salty seawater into fresh drinking water.

▼ OHIO-CLASS SUBMARINE

The U.S. Navy has 14 submarines that carry nuclear missiles. Those are called Ohio-class submarines. They are the largest submarines ever built by the United States. Each one is powered by a nuclear reactor.

Periscopes and radio aerials on top of the sail can be poked up above the surface of the sea.

These small "wings" are called hydroplanes. They tilt to make the submarine go up or down in the water.

The hull of the submarine is shaped to let it slip through the water easily. There is no deck. Sailors do not go outside much on a submarine!

726

PROJ

Ohio-class submarines have torpedoes to defend themselves. The torpedoes come out of these holes when they are fired.

Sub Power

Most attack subs use **diesel** engines. Those engines need air. They run only while the sub is above water. While underwater, subs are powered by batteries. Submarines must rise when the batteries run out.

Other submarines use nuclear power. A nuclear reactor heats water, turning it to steam. The steam spins **turbine** engines.

▼ CONTROL ROOM
A submarine has a large crew. Each of the sailors has an important job. Some run the engines or man the weapons. These sailors are in the control room. They steer the submarine and watch for enemies.

▲ LOADING A TORPEDO
Sailors load an anti-submarine torpedo into its
launcher aboard the USS *Arkansas*. Some ships carry
torpedoes that are designed only to sink submarines.

Those engines do not need air, so the subs
can stay underwater for a long time. All
missile subs use nuclear power. Some
attack subs do, too.

Life on a Sub

Working on a submarine is not easy. Even on
big subs, there is little room. Sailors might
not see daylight for two months.

Sailors get a lot of training to work on a
sub. They must know how all its parts
work. They must be prepared for

emergencies, such as fires and floods.
Sometimes, subs break down. Sailors get
trapped underwater. Then, rescue teams
have to find them.

CHAPTER 4

WARSHIPS

Navies use different kinds of warships for different jobs. Some are large. They have powerful weapons that can hit many targets. Others are smaller but faster. They can move in quickly for an attack.

Battleships were once the biggest warships of all time. They had huge guns and heavy armor for protection. After World War II (1939–1945), navies did not use them as much. They mostly used smaller warships. Today, battleships are not used at all.

▼ **LAST BATTLESHIP**
The U.S. Navy was the last to get rid of its battleships. Below are the guns of the USS *Missouri*. They fired huge shells a long way, but today's missiles can hit targets even farther away.

Big and Powerful

Cruisers are smaller than battleships, but they are still huge. They are longer than a football field! They are currently the world's largest warships.

Destroyers were once small ships. They protected bigger, slower ships from boats and subs. Today, they are almost as big as cruisers. In many navies, destroyers are the largest ships. They are fast and can move around easily.

Both kinds of ships have powerful guns. They can carry torpedoes and missiles. Ships may carry helicopters, too. They can hit targets on land, at sea, and in the air.

DID YOU KNOW?

The USS *Missouri* was the last U.S. battleship built. This huge ship fought in World War II. In 1991, it fought in the Persian Gulf War, firing missiles and guns at targets on land. Today, the ship is a museum at Pearl Harbor in Hawaii.

▼ **MISSILE CRUISER**
The USS *Mobile Bay* carries powerful missiles. It can fight other ships or shoot down aircraft. Some of its missiles can hit targets on land.

This cruiser has built-in radar. That lets the cruiser see many aircraft and ships at once. Computers keep track of them all.

Domes and **antennas** contain different sorts of radar. Some are used to track ships. Others follow aircraft in the sky.

Ready for Battle

Cruisers and destroyers have strong hulls built of thick steel. Inside the hulls are powerful gas turbine engines. With those engines, ships can travel long distances without refueling.

Up on deck, the ships have weapons for attack and for defense. Many carry a powerful gun called the Phalanx. If nothing else stops an enemy missile, that gun can blast it away.

Sailors need to know what is around them at all times. Besides sonar, they also use radar to detect enemies. Radar is similar to sonar, but it uses radio waves instead of sound waves. Radar finds enemy ships, planes, and missiles.

Small but Tough

Frigates are the smallest warships that travel at sea. They often protect larger ships carrying troops or supplies. Frigates may be small, but they carry powerful weapons.

Amphibious ships bring troops to land. Some are like small aircraft carriers. They carry special planes. Others can travel right onto land, letting out troops and vehicles. Navies also use **minesweepers**. Those ships search for enemy mines in the water.

▼ CHINESE VISITOR
This Chinese destroyer in California's San Diego Harbor was among the first Chinese warships that visited the United States.

Warships in Action

A warship may travel among a group of ships that protect aircraft carriers, or it may travel alone. Some warships hunt for submarines. Their helicopters find subs before they can attack. Other warships search for planes. They keep track of many planes at once and can hit them with missiles. Warships help troops by hitting targets on land.

Warships do other jobs, too. When disaster strikes, they may be the only help around. They can send helicopters or small boats to rescue people. They can also protect ships against pirates and other sea criminals.

▲ HELICOPTERS ON BOARD
Helicopters transport troops and move supplies. Some hunt for submarines and attack them. Helicopters also rescue people in danger.

IN THEIR OWN WORDS

"[At sea], we trained constantly to ensure both our equipment and our minds were ready for anything that came our way. Good maintenance, good training, and good information … were essential to ensure that readiness."

U.S. Navy Cmdr. Lisa Franchetti,
former captain of the USS *Ross*

CHAPTER 5

COAST GUARDS

Most countries have coast guards. In some countries, the coast guard is a part of the military. They defend coasts against enemy attack. In others, they are more like a police force or a rescue service.

All coast guards have one job in common. They help and protect people in coastal waters. Like navies, coast guards face tough challenges at sea.

Keeping the Oceans Safe

The U.S. Coast Guard is a part of the military, but it is separate from the Navy. The U.S. Coast Guard protects against attacks or invasions from the sea.

The U.S. Coast Guard has many other jobs, too. It enforces the law at sea. It searches for people in trouble and rescues them. The U.S. Coast Guard also protects the environment.

▼ ICE BREAKER
Some coastguard ships have to work where the sea freezes. They are special ships with strong hulls that can crash through the ice. They can rescue vessels that are stuck.

▼ ALL ABOARD!
Getting from a small boat to a big cargo ship means a long climb, but that is a typical job for members of the U.S. Coast Guard.

Large and Small

The U.S. Coast Guard uses many different types of boats and ships. The largest coast guard ships are called **cutters**. Some are as large as some navy ships. They also have powerful weapons.

High-endurance cutters are the biggest ships. They travel far out to sea. Medium-endurance cutters are smaller. They patrol closer to shore. The U.S. Coast Guard also uses planes and helicopters.

DID YOU KNOW?

The U.S. Navy cannot fire on a **civilian** ship that will not stop, but the U.S. Coast Guard can. If a boat does not stop, the U.S. Coast Guard snipers can shoot out its engine.

Joining the Fight

Sometimes, the U.S. Coast Guard helps with battles. During World War II, it protected ships that crossed the Atlantic Ocean. It also saved the lives of many soldiers.

U.S. Coast Guard ships help out all over the world. They may fight alongside Navy ships, or they may hit targets on land. The U.S. Coast Guard also fights pollution. It helps with oil spills and other disasters around the world.

DID YOU KNOW?

A Motor Life Boat (MLB) is much smaller than a cutter. It often finds and rescues people who are lost at sea. If it flips over, or **capsizes**, it flips back again on its own. It is almost unsinkable!

▼ A U.S. COAST GUARD RESPONSE BOAT
The U.S. Coast Guard does a dangerous job. Crews need the best equipment. This Response Boat is fast. It is also hard to sink and can operate in very bad weather.

U.S. Coast Guard in Action

In 2004, a dramatic rescue took place. Off the coast of Alaska, a ship was caught in a bad storm. U.S. Coast Guard helicopters and a cutter went out to rescue the crew.

Winds were fierce. A helicopter crashed into the sea during the rescue, but the U.S. Coast Guard crew brought most of the people to safety.

The ship broke in half. It spilled thousands of gallons of oil into the water. After the rescue, the U.S. Coast Guard helped clean up the oil spill.

▲ AFTER THE STORM
This cargo ship, the *Selendang Ayu*, was carrying soybeans from Seattle, Washington, to China. It ran aground off the coast of Alaska. U.S. Coast Guard helicopters rescued most of the crew.

IN THEIR OWN WORDS

"We did another quick sweep of the vessel to make sure that it wasn't sinking .... We found another automatic weapon that hadn't been found before."

U.S. Coast Guard Damage Controlman 3rd Class Nathan Bruckenthal, team member during Operation Iraqi Freedom

GLOSSARY

aircraft carriers—large ships with flat decks that airplanes use for taking off and landing

amphibious—describes a type of military ship that can carry troops and supplies from sea to land; describes something that is adapted to both land and water

antennas—devices that detect or send radio signals

ballast tanks—on a submarine, tanks that fill with air to make it float or fill with water to make it dive

camouflaged—giving something the same shape or colors as its surroundings, so it blends in and is hard to see

capsizes—turns upside down in the water

catapults—on aircraft carriers, devices that help an airplane to take off by pushing it rapidly down the deck

civilian—describing a type of nonmilitary ship that may or may not be used by the military during a time of war or peace

cutters—in a coast guard, the largest and most powerful ships

decoys—fake targets designed to fool enemy torpedoes; torpedoes hit the decoys instead of a ship

demolition—the process of destroying something

diesel—a kind of engine fuel that is similar to gasoline

fleet—a large group of Navy ships under the command of one officer; a fleet is usually put together for a specific job, such as patrolling a certain part of the world

hull—the main part of a ship or boat, including the sides and bottom

hydroplanes—on a submarine, small wing-like flaps that are used to control how steeply a submarine dives or rises

insignia—the markings on a uniform that tell the rank of a service member

minesweepers—special ships used by a navy to detect mines, or explosives that are hidden underwater

nuclear power—a type of energy created by splitting atoms of certain chemical elements

periscope—on a submarine, a device that lets sailors see on the surface while they are underwater

radar—a system that uses radio waves to find things; radar sends out radio waves that bounce against something and come back

rank—the position of a person in the military; on a U.S. Navy ship, everyone follows the orders of the captain, who is of highest rank

sail—on a submarine, a tower on top of the ship that holds the periscope and radio antennas

simulator—a device that lets people pretend to do something, such as work on a ship, in order to provide training

sonar—a system that uses sound to find things underwater by sending out pulses of sound that bounce against something and come back

submarine—a kind of ship that can travel deep underwater for long periods of time

supercarrier—a very large aircraft carrier that can hold many airplanes

torpedo—a weapon that travels underwater to a target and then explodes

turbine—a fan-like wheel in an engine; when a gas such as steam rushes past a turbine, the turbine spins, creating power

FOR MORE INFORMATION

Books

Naval Warship: FSF-1 Sea Fighter.
Steve White (Children's Press, 2007)

Navy Seals in Action. Special Ops (series).
Nel Yomtov (Bearport Publishing, 2008)

Navy Ships in Action. Amazing Military
Vehicles (series). Kay Jackson
(Rosen Publishing, 2009)

Nimitz Aircraft Carriers. Torque Military
Machines (series). Derek Zobel
(Children's Press, 2008)

Submarines Up Close. Up Close (series). Andra
Serlin Abramson (Sterling, 2008)

U.S. Coast Guard Cutters. Blazers (series).
Carrie A. Braulick (Capstone Press, 2006)

Web Sites

Carnegie Science Center:
How a Submarine Dives and Surfaces
www.carnegiesciencecenter.org/Default.aspx?
pageId=62
Learn more about how submarines dive and
surface—and also find instructions for a
science project.

How Stuff Works:
Aircraft Carriers
www.science.howstuffworks.com/aircraft-carrier.htm
Discover how aircraft carriers work and see
many great photos of sailors in action.

Navy SEALs: Image Gallery
www.sealchallenge.navy.mil/seal/imagegallery.aspx
Visit this site to see photos of Navy SEALs in
action around the world.

Popular Mechanics:
Wreck of the Selendang Ayu
www.popularmechanics.com/technology/transporta
tion/1641371.html?page=1
Explore photos and information about the
rescue of the *Selendang Ayu* by the
U.S. Coast Guard.

U.S. Navy Ships
www.navy.mil/navydata/our_ships.asp
Learn more about the different kinds of ships
used by the U.S. Navy.

INDEX

ABOUT THE AUTHOR

Martin J. Dougherty holds a Bachelor of Education degree from the University of Sunderland in the United Kingdom. He has taught throughout northeast England and his published work includes books on subjects as diverse as space exploration, martial arts, and military hardware. He is an expert on missile systems and low-intensity warfare.